A Gift For

_____

From

_____

STRENGTH *for the* SOUL *from* OUR DAILY BREAD

Hope

Discovery House Publishers

Books, music, and videos that feed the soul with the Word of God

Box 3566 Grand Rapids, MI 49501

Interior design by Sherri L. Hoffman

Printed in Italy

06 07 08 09 / L.E.G.O. / 10 9 8 7 6 5 4 3 2 1

Introduction

*S*ince April 1956, millions of readers around the world have found daily inspiration, hope, comfort, and biblical truth from the pages of *Our Daily Bread*. Now you can find encouragement from one of the most beloved devotionals on the subject of hope, compiled into one convenient volume.

We believe that this book will be of help to you and those you know in every circumstance of life. May it and the Word of God bring strength to your soul.

Other books in the Strength for the Soul
from *Our Daily Bread* series

Comfort
Grief
Peace
Prayer
Trust

A Sure Hope

And now, dear children, continue in him, so that when he appears we may be confident and unashamed before him at his coming. If you know that he is righteous, you know that everyone who does what is right has been born of him. . . .

How great is the love the Father has lavished on us, that we should be called children of God! And that is what we are! The reason the world does not know us is that it did not know him. Dear friends, now we are children of God, and what we will be has not yet been made known. But we know that when he appears, we shall be like him, for we shall see him as he is. Everyone who has this hope in him purifies himself, just as he is pure.

—1 JOHN 2:28-29; 3:1-3

used to be embarrassed by the so-called Christian concept of hope. But now I realize my embarrassment stemmed from an idea I just thought was Christian. To me the word "hope" suggested merely wishing, and that seemed like a weak, almost superstitious way to face the future. I've come to understand that hope, in the biblical sense, is much more than just wanting something to happen. It implies certainty and involves confidence and a real sense of expectancy.

I thought of this while reading about some household pets that become greatly disturbed by their owner's prolonged absence. When temporarily placed in a boarding kennel, it's possible for them to have a heart attack. Or they become so upset that they actually die from nervous exhaustion or from just giving up. As a result, pet owners who are planning to leave their animals for a period of time are encouraged to give them "hope" by first helping them to "believe" that they will return. This can be done by occasionally boarding the dog or cat for just a day or two to prepare it for longer absences.

These experiences teach the pet to expect its master to come back. They can actually save its life. This is similar to what Christ did for His disciples. After temporarily leaving them in death, He rejoined them three days later. Then, in a rather unpredictable manner, He appeared and reappeared over the next forty days. When He left them for the last time and ascended to Glory, it was only after He had given His followers good reason for the sure hope of His final return.

—MART DE HAAN

The God of Hope

For you have been my hope, O Sovereign LORD,
  my confidence since my youth.
From birth I have relied on you;
  you brought me forth from my mother's womb.
  I will ever praise you.
I have become like a portent to many,
  but you are my strong refuge.
My mouth is filled with your praise,
  declaring your splendor all day long.

—PSALM 71:5–8

In his book *Man's Search for Meaning*, Dr. Viktor E. Frankl recounts a moving personal experience he had in a German concentration camp during World War II.

> I was struggling to find the reason for my suffering, my slow dying. In a last violent protest against the hopelessness of imminent death, I sensed my spirit piercing through the enveloping gloom. I felt it transcend that hopeless, meaningless world, and from somewhere I heard a victorious yes in answer to my question of the existence of an ultimate purpose. At that moment a light was lit in a distant farmhouse which stood on the horizon as if painted there, in the midst of the miserable gray of a dawning morning in Bavaria.

Ever since sin brought suffering into the world, God has been saying a resounding yes to man's search for meaning amid the seeming absurdities of life. He reassured Adam and Eve in their helplessness and shame. He encouraged Abraham when He told him he would become the father of many nations. He cheered Israel again and again through the promise of a coming Savior. Then after Jesus died on the cross for our sins, God again said yes by raising Him from the dead. Today His Holy Spirit instills hope in the heart of every suffering one who turns to Christ.

Has life become empty for you? Then voice the psalmist's prayer, "You have been my hope, O Sovereign LORD."

—DENNIS DE HAAN

Filled with Hope

Who shall separate us from the love of Christ? Shall trouble or hardship or persecution or famine or nakedness or danger or sword? As it is written:

> "For your sake we face death all day long;
> we are considered as sheep to be slaughtered."

No, in all these things we are more than conquerors through him who loved us. For I am convinced that neither death nor life, neither angels nor demons, neither the present nor the future, nor any powers, neither height nor depth, nor anything else in all creation, will be able to separate us from the love of God that is in Christ Jesus our Lord. —ROMANS 8:35–39

*M*an's greatest need in adversity is hope. If the light of anticipation grows dim and finally goes out, the darkness of apathy and despair sets in. But a continuing strong sense of expectancy will enable us to bear any pain, any trial.

A newsboy, thinly clad and drenched to the skin by the soaking rain, stood shivering in the doorway one cold day in November. Every few minutes his shrill cry could be heard, "Morning papers! Morning papers!" A gentleman, who was well protected by his coat and umbrella, stopped to buy the early edition. Noticing the boy's discomfort, he said, "This kind of weather is pretty hard on you, isn't it?" Looking up with a cheery smile, the youngster replied, "I don't mind too much, Mister. The sun will shine again!"

Christians can have the same confidence. The apostle Paul wrote, "Now may the God of hope fill you with all joy and peace in believing, that you may abound in hope" (Romans 15:13 NKJV). He could say this because Jesus Christ had come into the world to pay sin's penalty and conquer death. Through faith in Him, Paul shared in the very life of God Himself. Earlier in Romans he cited every hope-destroying contingency known to man, including life, death, angels, principalities, powers, things present, things to come, height, depth, and any other creation. His conclusion? Nothing can separate us from the love of God!

If you are suffering, you can be filled with hope by trusting the God of hope. —Dennis De Haan

11

A Realistic Hope

For the grace of God that brings salvation has appeared to all men. It teaches us to say "No" to ungodliness and worldly passions, and to live self-controlled, upright and godly lives in this present age, while we wait for the blessed hope—the glorious appearing of our great God and Savior, Jesus Christ, who gave himself for us to redeem us from all wickedness and to purify for himself a people that are his very own, eager to do what is good.

—TITUS 2:11–14

The other day I met an elderly preacher friend who gave me his "calling card." It read: "No business, no phone, no address, no money. Retired, but Titus 2:13." Though his health is not the best and his income is meager, he is content and optimistic. Eagerly anticipating "the glorious appearing" of Jesus Christ, he is not engaging in mere wishful thinking. His expectation has a solid basis in experience and fact, for in his own personal life he knows the reality of deliverance from sin's guilt and power. He has received answers to prayer, and strength for each day. He trusts the Bible and is convinced that the Savior literally rose from the grave. That's why he has the calm assurance expressed in the gentle humor of his "calling card."

How different is the outlook of non-Christians! Many have simply abandoned all hope and are living in quiet despair. One man, for example, said to me bitterly, "Don't try to tell me about God and eternal life. When a person dies, that's the end. The only place anyone goes is six feet under." Regarding the prospects for mankind, most of the world's leading thinkers see the future filled with insurmountable difficulties, which will terminate in total oblivion. Those who do promise a world of peace and plenty, or a lovely afterlife, offer no support for their dreams. They are doing little more than whistling in the dark, and they know it.

If you want something to look forward to, admit your sin and accept Jesus Christ as your personal Savior. He will save you and give you a realistic hope. —HERB VANDER LUGT

13

Hope—or Wishful Thinking?

For whatever things were written before were written for our learning, that we through the patience and comfort of the Scriptures might have hope. Now may the God of patience and comfort grant you to be like-minded toward one another, according to Christ Jesus, that you may with one mind and one mouth glorify the God and Father of our Lord Jesus Christ. . . .

Now may the God of hope fill you with all joy and peace in believing, that you may abound in hope by the power of the Holy Spirit. —Romans 15:4–6, 13 (NKJV)

The hope spoken of in the Bible is actually faith looking forward with joyous anticipation. Some people, though, use this beautiful word to describe an expectation that is nothing more than wishful thinking. Recently I heard a non-Christian psychologist stress the importance of instilling hope in the mind of a terminally ill person. I wondered if he believed in life after death, and I soon discovered that he didn't. All he could offer was the tentative prospect of a few added years.

A dying person who has nothing to look forward to beyond this life may find some comfort in thinking that he has a little more time. But eventually he must resign himself to the inevitable and face death. The one who does not know God through Christ has no basis for optimism about eternity. That's why the apostle Paul spoke of the heathen nations of the Old Testament era as "without hope and without God in the world" (Ephesians 2:12).

How different when a person knows the Lord! I remember visiting a friend who had just learned that he had inoperable cancer. He wasn't protesting and saying that the doctors were wrong. He wasn't rebellious or angry with God. On the contrary, he was confident that his future was in the Lord's hands.

Romans 15:4 says that God gives us hope through the Scriptures. And Paul's prayer in verse 13 intimates that this virtue becomes a reality "in believing." So if you want to "abound in hope," study the Bible and exercise your faith. Don't settle for mere wishful thinking!   —Herb Vander Lugt

On the Winning Side

Then I saw a new heaven and a new earth, for the first heaven and the first earth had passed away, and there was no longer any sea. I saw the Holy City, the new Jerusalem, coming down out of heaven from God, prepared as a bride beautifully dressed for her husband. And I heard a loud voice from the throne saying, "Now the dwelling of God is with men, and he will live with them. They will be his people, and God himself will be with them and be their God. He will wipe every tear from their eyes. There will be no more death or mourning or crying or pain, for the old order of things has passed away."

He who was seated on the throne said, "I am making everything new!" Then he said, "Write this down, for these words are trustworthy and true."

He said to me: "It is done. I am the Alpha and the Omega, the Beginning and the End. To him who is thirsty I will give to drink without cost from the spring of the water of life. He who overcomes will inherit all this, and I will be his God and he will be my son."

—Revelation 21:1–7

One of the strongest incentives for victorious Christian living is the confidence that God will have the final word in the struggle between good and evil. We know that we will someday be delivered not only from the penalty of sin but also from its presence and power. This encourages us to press on in our battle against the forces of darkness. An old Christian gentleman who was known for his optimistic outlook was asked the secret of his triumphant attitude. He replied, "I've read the last book of the Bible, so I know how the story ends. I'm on the winning side!"

A Little Leaguer was playing the outfield in the first game of the season. After chasing a long hit and hustling the ball back into the infield, someone asked him how his team was doing and what the score was. The youngster replied that his team was doing well, but that they were trailing 17–0. The bystander asked if he was discouraged at being so far behind, and if he was ready to admit defeat. He came back immediately with this retort: "We aren't beat—we haven't even been up to bat yet!"

Hope is a vital element also in the battle with sin. We have good reason for confidence because God is in heaven and all power rests in Him. And all who serve Him can draw on His unlimited resources. Let that sure prospect encourage you to be more than a conqueror through Him who loves you. Take heart. In the power of the indwelling Spirit, resist temptation. Obey God's Word. Remember, you're on the winning side!

—RICHARD DE HAAN

Where Is He?

Hasten, O God, to save me;
  O LORD, come quickly to help me.
May those who seek my life
  be put to shame and confusion;
may all who desire my ruin
  be turned back in disgrace.
May those who say to me, "Aha! Aha!"
  turn back because of their shame.
But may all who seek you
  rejoice and be glad in you;
may those who love your salvation always say,
  "Let God be exalted!"

Yet I am poor and needy;
  come quickly to me, O God.
You are my help and my deliverer;
  O Lord, do not delay.   —PSALM 70:1–5

The *Detroit Free Press* printed the letter of one of the captives held as a hostage in Iran. He was sixty-four years old and was writing on the twenty-fourth day of his imprisonment. Here's what he said to a friend back home who had been assuring him of her prayers: "I wish I could have your faith. But unfortunately I don't, and with the length of time that this matter has been going on, I think none of the prayers offered are being heard. As you know, I have traveled a good deal in this world and have visited the sites of former concentration camps where millions of people suffered horribly and died. Their supplications were not heard. So how can one continue to have faith?"

He had a point. You can convince yourself that God is going to change your circumstances, but that doesn't mean He will. That's why it's so important to understand the kind of help God offers us in His Word. People who do not have a personal knowledge of Him have no real hope—not in this world nor in the world to come. But the child of God can always have hope and encouragement like David expressed in Psalm 70. David was confident that the Lord could change his circumstances. But even if that didn't happen, he knew the Lord would not abandon him to the grave (Psalm 16:10). He believed that even if God in His wisdom chose not to give him what he wanted in this life, He would not disappoint him in the next.

We need that same assurance. God can rescue now. But if He doesn't, it's because He has a better plan.

—MART DE HAAN

Looking Up When You're Down

My soul thirsts for God, for the living God.
When can I go and meet with God?
My tears have been my food
day and night,
while men say to me all day long,
"Where is your God?"
These things I remember
as I pour out my soul:
how I used to go with the multitude,
leading the procession to the house of God,
with shouts of joy and thanksgiving
among the festive throng.

Why are you downcast, O my soul?
Why so disturbed within me?
Put your hope in God,
for I will yet praise him,
my Savior and my God.

—PSALM 42:2–5

We all have those moments in life when we're down. We get the "blues." Nothing looks right to us. Everything seems to be going wrong. And to make matters worse, no solution or relief is in sight. Speaking out of his own experience, the psalmist cried, "Why are you downcast, O my soul? Why so disturbed within me? Put your hope in God." That's good advice for anyone who is facing discouragement.

In the book of Acts we are told about an experience in the life of the apostle Paul while he was on board ship en route to Rome. A violent storm threatened to plunge the vessel and all its passengers to the bottom of the sea. One night, however, an angel of the Lord appeared and assured the apostle that not a person on board would perish. Paul believed that message and said to his fellow passengers, "Take heart, men, for I believe God that it will be just as it was told me" (Acts 27:25 NKJV). Like the psalmist in today's Scripture reading, Paul's hope was in the Lord.

Even though you may be fearful and disheartened, you can find reason for cheer if you look to the heavenly Father. Remember what the psalmist advised, "Put your hope in God," and then say with the apostle Paul, "I believe God."

You may be thinking, "That was all right for him because he had a promise from the Lord. But what have I got?" Have you forgotten Philippians 4:19? Read it again. Believe it. And the next time you're down, remember to look up!

—RICHARD DE HAAN

God Is for Us!

"'But you, O mountains of Israel, will produce branches and fruit for my people Israel, for they will soon come home. I am concerned for you and will look on you with favor; you will be plowed and sown, and I will multiply the number of people upon you, even the whole house of Israel. The towns will be inhabited and the ruins rebuilt. I will increase the number of men and animals upon you, and they will be fruitful and become numerous. I will settle people on you as in the past and will make you prosper more than before. Then you will know that I am the LORD. I will cause people, my people Israel, to walk upon you. They will possess you, and you will be their inheritance; you will never again deprive them of their children.'"

—EZEKIEL 36:8–12

Have you ever felt as if you were on the losing team? I'm not talking about baseball, football, or basketball. I'm referring to the game of life in which the penalties for being offside or out-of-bounds can really set us back. What makes this game so discouraging, though, is that we often lose ground because of our own foolish mistakes—those sins we could have avoided.

Many Jews must have felt that way about their plight after mighty Babylon had taken Israel captive. The land lay desolate. Jerusalem had become a dusty heap of charred timbers and displaced stones. The nobles and princes had been carried away to die in a foreign land, and the few people left in the rubble were forced to live in poverty and misery. The nation was reaping the bitter fruits of wickedness and idolatry. Yet God had not abandoned His people. In a strange but pointed command the Lord told His servant Ezekiel to prophesy to the mountains of Israel, "Indeed I am for you, and I will turn to you" (Ezekiel 36:9 NKJV). To a despairing Jew, those words must have kindled hope. Although he might never see the day himself, he was reassured that Jehovah would restore the nation.

As Christians, we too have a message from the Lord that can keep us on the winning side. Paul stated it in Romans 8:31: "If God is for us, who can be against us?" When the dark consequences of our sin and failure engulf us, this truth can renew within our hearts a hope that is steadfast and sure. God is for us—that's a thought equal to life's most discouraging times!

—DENNIS DE HAAN

23

The Cross of Hope

Praise be to the God and Father of our Lord Jesus Christ! In his great mercy he has given us new birth into a living hope through the resurrection of Jesus Christ from the dead, and into an inheritance that can never perish, spoil or fade—kept in heaven for you, who through faith are shielded by God's power until the coming of the salvation that is ready to be revealed in the last time. In this you greatly rejoice, though now for a little while you may have had to suffer grief in all kinds of trials. These have come so that your faith—of greater worth than gold, which perishes even though refined by fire—may be proved genuine and may result in praise, glory and honor when Jesus Christ is revealed. Though you have not seen him, you love him; and even though you do not see him now, you believe in him and are filled with an inexpressible and glorious joy for you are receiving the goal of your faith, the salvation of your souls. —1 PETER 1:3–9

As Christians, we are sometimes called upon to suffer. But whether our affliction comes from those who despise and oppose us, or from illness or hardship, we can find great encouragement and hope when we think of the agony our Lord endured. Peter said that Christ suffered for us, leaving us an example (1 Peter 2:21). The Savior's willing submission to the cross gives us strength to go on.

In recounting his experiences as a political prisoner in Russia, Alexander Solzhenitsyn tells of a moment when he was on the verge of giving up all hope. He was forced to work twelve hours a day at hard labor while existing on a starvation diet, and he had become gravely ill. The doctors were predicting his death. One afternoon, while shoveling sand under a blazing sun, he simply stopped working. He did so even though he knew the guards would beat him severely—perhaps to death. But he felt that he just couldn't go on. Then he saw another prisoner, a fellow Christian, moving toward him cautiously. With his cane the man quickly drew a cross in the sand and erased it. In that brief moment, Solzhenitsyn felt all of the hope of the gospel flood through his soul. It gave him courage to endure that difficult day and the months of imprisonment that followed.

Perhaps you are encountering opposition, physical pain, or mental anguish, and you feel like giving up. If so, look to the One who died on Calvary. His suffering will bring you renewed strength and grace. For every believer, the cross is indeed the cross of hope.

—DAVE EGNER

The Christian Hope

"All my intimate friends detest me;
>   those I love have turned against me.
I am nothing but skin and bones;
>   I have escaped with only the skin of my teeth. . . .

"Oh, that my words were recorded,
>   that they were written on a scroll,
that they were inscribed with an iron tool on lead,
>   or engraved in rock forever!
I know that my Redeemer lives,
>   and that in the end he will stand upon the earth.
And after my skin has been destroyed,
>   yet in my flesh I will see God;
I myself will see him
>   with my own eyes—I, and not another.
>   How my heart yearns within me!

—JOB 19:19–20, 23–27

A child of God can rise above every trouble and trial of life if he anticipates the glories of heaven and the joy of being there with his Savior.

I received a letter from a severely handicapped man who possessed the sense of victory that comes through this forward look of faith. He had survived a long, delicate cranial operation, but he suffered some brain damage, partial blindness, a high degree of deafness, and mild paralysis. In addition, he spent several months on dialysis after both kidneys failed. He went through an unsuccessful transplant operation and endured another period on dialysis before receiving a replacement kidney. He admitted that he felt pretty low at times, but he didn't stay down in the dumps. This man fully believed that God has a loving purpose in everything He allows, and he said he was looking forward to the glorified body awaiting him. He closed his letter by saying, "I can live with my problems, because I know all of these things are preparing me for heaven."

In our Scripture lesson, we read not only of Job's bitter lament, but also of his beautiful expression of hope. He bewailed his loneliness, for in addition to losing his wealth, his sons and daughters, and his health, he had been abandoned by everyone. Even little children would have nothing to do with him. Yet he found consolation! Deep within, he believed that on the other side of death he would see God as His Friend and Savior. With that hope he could triumph over everything—and so can we!

—HERB VANDER LUGT

The Best Hope of All

Paul, a servant of God and an apostle of Jesus Christ for the faith of God's elect and the knowledge of the truth that leads to godliness—a faith and knowledge resting on the hope of eternal life, which God, who does not lie, promised before the beginning of time, and at his appointed season he brought his word to light through the preaching entrusted to me by the command of God our Savior. —TITUS 1:1–3

Medical doctors and psychologists agree that hope is vital to physical and mental health. This was borne out recently when a surgeon postponed an operation because his patient felt sure he was going to die on the operating table. Studies of prisoners of war also verify the importance of hope. Apparently, strong men who lose all expectation of release are more likely to die than their physically weaker companions who are more optimistic.

If hope has such great value when it relates to the things of this life, think of what it can do for a person if it encompasses both time and eternity. I saw this firsthand when I talked to an aged believer who knew he was soon going to die. He had already endured major stomach surgery, the amputation of a leg, and a disabling stroke. He couldn't talk very clearly, but he managed to say to me, "Brother, each of those blows has been a boost. Each one has drawn me closer to Christ and made me more eager for heaven." Another man, a recent convert who appears to be losing his battle against cancer, assured me that while he still hopes medical science will find a cure, he is also looking forward expectantly to seeing his Savior when he enters Glory. The world has no match for that kind of anticipation.

The Christian's hope is superior. It is based on the death of Jesus for our sins and His resurrection from the grave. We are assured of victory in this life and a glorious eternity in the next. That's why it's called a "living hope." —HERB VANDER LUGT

Begin the Day
with Hope

O LORD, how many are my foes!
  How many rise up against me!
Many are saying of me,
  "God will not deliver him."

Selah

But you are a shield around me, O LORD;
  you bestow glory on me and lift up my head. . . .

I lie down and sleep;
  I wake again, because the LORD sustains me.
I will not fear the tens of thousands
  drawn up against me on every side.

—PSALM 3:1–3, 5–6

While we usually wake up each morning anticipating the activities of a new day, sometimes we experience feelings of dread. After a night of fitful sleep, we may feel ill-equipped to face the problems we expect to encounter. Dark, depressing thoughts can quickly overwhelm us.

If anyone had reason to feel like that, it was David when he composed Psalm 3. He and a small band of followers had been driven from the palace in Jerusalem because of a rebellion staged by his own son Absalom. They had spent the first night fording the Jordan River, had made camp the next day, and had retired on the second night with the problem still unresolved. Even so, David was able to lie down and go to sleep. When he awoke in the morning, the thought of the great odds against him came to mind (v. 1), but he didn't entertain it long. Instead, he looked upward in faith to God, backward in gratitude for His mercies, and forward in expectation of His mighty deliverance. Thus he could enter the new day with hope.

Some mornings we wake up to a very difficult day. When this happens, we can either give in to despair or follow the example of David. Faith, gratitude, and expectation will enable us to face the most trying day with strong confidence in God.

—HERB VANDER LUGT

Looking for Hope?

My soul is downcast within me;
   therefore I will remember you
   from the land of the Jordan,
   the heights of Hermon—from Mount Mizar. . . .

By day the LORD directs his love,
   at night his song is with me—
   a prayer to the God of my life.

I say to God my Rock,
   "Why have you forgotten me?
Why must I go about mourning,
   oppressed by the enemy?"
My bones suffer mortal agony
   as my foes taunt me,
saying to me all day long,
   "Where is your God?"

Why are you downcast, O my soul?
   Why so disturbed within me?
Put your hope in God,
   for I will yet praise him,
   my Savior and my God.   —PSALM 42:6, 8–11

A missionary in India lay burning with the fever of malaria. As the disease sapped her strength, a feeling of depression dragged her into the depths of despair. She felt so overwhelmed that she asked God to take her to heaven. But one day, while enclosed in this cocoon of discouragement, the sounds of music drifted into her room from another part of the house. A group of Indian young people were having a worship service. She heard them sing in their dialect, "I have decided to follow Jesus; no turning back, no turning back." The song touched her heart and she began praying. Soon prayer graduated to praise, and God lifted her discouragement. Not long afterward, her health returned. Now, many years later, she continues effectively in the task of world missions.

Can you relate to her experience? Have you known the kind of discouragement that can make you want to give up? Have you felt such a burden of depression that you have raised David's question, "Why are you cast down, O my soul? And why are you disquieted within me?" (Psalm 42:11 NKJV).

Whenever you start to get down, remember that David had not only the problem but also the solution. "Hope in God," he said. The encouragement of God's presence will bring praise to your heart and renewed faithfulness to your walk. Sing from your deepest being, "I have decided to follow Jesus; no turning back, no turning back." When you trust Jesus, you'll find hope.

—PAUL VAN GORDER

When Dreams Don't Come True

This is what the LORD Almighty, the God of Israel, says to all those I carried into exile from Jerusalem to Babylon: "Build houses and settle down; plant gardens and eat what they produce. Marry and have sons and daughters; find wives for your sons and give your daughters in marriage, so that they too may have sons and daughters. Increase in number there; do not decrease. Also, seek the peace and prosperity of the city to which I have carried you into exile. Pray to the LORD for it, because if it prospers, you too will prosper." Yes, this is what the LORD Almighty, the God of Israel, says: "Do not let the prophets and diviners among you deceive you. . . . They are prophesying lies to you in my name. I have not sent them," declares the LORD. . . .

"For I know the plans I have for you," declares the LORD, "plans to prosper you and not to harm you, plans to give you hope and a future."

*—*JEREMIAH 29:4–9, 11

Shattered dreams! It happens all the time. A man dies unexpectedly just before retirement, leaving his wife to face conditions far different from those of which she had dreamed. A young man is an outstanding baseball pitcher in college. He does well in tryouts with a major league team and anticipates becoming a professional. But his hopes are suddenly dashed when he is told that his fastball isn't quite up to standard.

Shattered dreams! These words aptly describe what happened to a large group of Jewish people in 597 BC. They were uprooted from their land and transported to Babylon as exiles. It appeared that all their hopes were gone. But before long, some false prophets told them that God would intervene and bring about their return very quickly if they would resist their captors. The people started dreaming again. Their hopes were high! But along came Jeremiah and shattered their dreams by telling them the prophets had been lying to them. He declared that the Lord planned on keeping them in Babylon for seventy years. Jeremiah said that if they would cooperate with their captors and become exemplary citizens they would discover that God's plan was for their good. They simply needed to trust Him to work it out (see Jeremiah 29:1–14).

It's good to dream big dreams and to do all we can to realize them. But when they don't come true, let's turn our eyes to God in humble trust. His plans are always best!

—HERB VANDER LUGT

Rejoicing in Hope

Therefore, since we have been justified through faith, we have peace with God through our Lord Jesus Christ, through whom we have gained access by faith into this grace in which we now stand. And we rejoice in the hope of the glory of God. Not only so, but we also rejoice in our sufferings, because we know that suffering produces perseverance; perseverance, character; and character, hope. And hope does not disappoint us, because God has poured out his love into our hearts by the Holy Spirit, whom he has given us. —ROMANS 5:1–5

The glories that await the Christian defy our comprehension. What we can grasp about them, however, fills us with great anticipation. We look longingly to that day when we shall enjoy heaven in all its fullness.

In his book *Dare to Believe,* Dan Baumann illustrates this unique experience of knowing that something is ours, yet longing to enjoy it more fully. He explains that at Christmastime he would always do a lot of snooping, trying to find the gift-wrapped presents and figure out what was in them. One year he discovered a package with his name on it that was easy to identify. There was no way to disguise the golf clubs inside. Baumann then made this observation: "When Mom wasn't around, I would go and feel the package, shake it, and pretend that I was on the golf course. The point is, I was already enjoying the pleasures of a future event; namely, the unveiling. It had my name on it. I knew what it was. But only Christmas would reveal it in its fullness."

That's the way it is with us as believers as we await what God has for us in heaven. Says Baumann, "We shall be glorified, but we are beginning to taste glorification now . . . This quality of life begins the moment an individual places faith in Christ and thereby shares His life. We have eternal life—here and now—but it is only a foretaste of its fullness. God has whetted our appetites for the main course, which has to come later!"

Yes, there's reason for rejoicing in hope!

—RICHARD DE HAAN

There Is Hope!

Elijah was afraid and ran for his life. When he came to Beersheba in Judah, he left his servant there, while he himself went a day's journey into the desert. He came to a broom tree, sat down under it and prayed that he might die. "I have had enough, Lord," he said. "Take my life; I am no better than my ancestors." Then he lay down under the tree and fell asleep.

All at once an angel touched him and said, "Get up and eat." He looked around, and there by his head was a cake of bread baked over hot coals, and a jar of water. He ate and drank and then lay down again.

The angel of the Lord came back a second time and touched him and said, "Get up and eat, for the journey is too much for you." So he got up and ate and drank. Strengthened by that food, he traveled forty days and forty nights until he reached Horeb, the mountain of God. There he went into a cave and spent the night.

And the word of the Lord came to him. —1 Kings 19:3–9

The letter that came to RBC Ministries bore no signature and no return address. It read, "By the time you receive this letter, I will have committed suicide. I accepted Christ two years ago. Lately my world has been crumbling around me. I can't take it anymore. I can't fall again or be 'bad' anymore. God and I have drifted apart . . . Lord, help me. Could you take a moment and say a prayer for me, a teenager? Lord, forgive me!"

Can Christians actually get that desperate? Most certainly! Read today's Scripture. Elijah was so physically and emotionally exhausted that he asked God to take his life. While that's not suicide, such a request does arise from the same feelings of despair. But God lifted him up! How? By strengthening him with food, restoring him through sleep, listening to his complaint, gently correcting him, reassuring him in a still, small voice, giving him new work to do, and telling him that all was not lost. That brought Elijah out of his depression.

Most people who take their own lives do so when they are deeply depressed. Reality becomes distorted and they can't see the selfish, sinful nature of their act. But God wants to restore and uphold them. Sometimes He speaks hope directly to the soul, but more often He uses sensitive, caring people who come alongside to help. Let's be God's hope to others today. A word, a smile, a helping hand—all say to those who are cast down, "In Christ there is hope." —DENNIS DE HAAN

Renewed Hope

This is the word that came to Jeremiah from the LORD: "Go down to the potter's house, and there I will give you my message." So I went down to the potter's house, and I saw him working at the wheel. But the pot he was shaping from the clay was marred in his hands; so the potter formed it into another pot, shaping it as seemed best to him.

Then the word of the LORD came to me: "O house of Israel, can I not do with you as this potter does?" declares the LORD. "Like clay in the hand of the potter, so are you in my hand, O house of Israel."   —JEREMIAH 18:1–6

Writing in *The Reaper,* Joanie Yoder told of reaching a point of despair in her role as a pastor's wife. She cited some of the stresses she faced: sharing her husband twenty-four hours a day, resenting perfectionist standards, feeling guilty about recurring bitterness and anger, and having no one with whom to share her feelings. Gradually she became so discouraged that she was ready to give up. Then something happened.

One day I opened my sorely neglected Bible to the writings of the prophet Jeremiah . . . I watched over Jeremiah's shoulder as the potter worked a lump of clay on his wheel. I began to get emotionally involved when the clay became marred in the potter's hand. Between the lines I assumed the potter would toss aside the lump of spoiled clay to take up another, hoping for better results . . . My life was that lump of clay, and I felt the old nagging fear that God, like this potter, might lay aside my disappointing life and take up another to do His work. But . . . I read on to see what the potter really did with the clay: "and he reworked it into another vessel, as it seemed good for the potter to do!" As if written for me alone, the next verse read, "Can I not do with you as this potter has done? says the Lord. Behold, like the clay in the potter's hand, so are you in My hand."

With renewed hope, Joanie realized that God was molding her for His use. What confidence this can give us!

—DAVE EGNER

God's Last Words

"Remember the Law of Moses, My servant, which I commanded him in Horeb for all Israel, with the statutes and judgments.

"Behold, I will send you Elijah the prophet before the coming of the great and dreadful day of the LORD. And he will turn the hearts of the fathers to the children, and the hearts of the children to their fathers, lest I come and strike the earth with a curse."

—MALACHI 4:4–6

*L*ast words are powerful words. Today's text expresses God's final words to Israel under the Old Testament dispensation. For four hundred years He would remain silent until they would hear "the voice of one crying in the wilderness: 'Prepare the way of the LORD' " (Matthew 3:3). Although Malachi 4:6 appears to be a curse, it really is not. It does not close the door on hope. On the contrary, it was God's last appeal of love. The threat of a curse, expressed by the word *lest*, was aimed at averting the natural consequence of disobedience.

G. Campbell Morgan noted that from Malachi's time until Christ's, rabbis did not end their reading of Malachi with verse six. Skipping from verse 4 to verse 6, they then reverted to verse 5, "Behold, I will send you Elijah the prophet before the coming of the great and dreadful day of the LORD." And in the Greek Old Testament the fourth verse is put at the end. Thus the Jews regarded God's final words as spoken in love, not in anger.

God's final words to believers in the New Testament are also filled with hope: "He who testifies to these things says, 'Surely I am coming quickly.' Amen. Even so, come, Lord Jesus! The grace of our Lord Jesus Christ be with you all. Amen" (Revelation 22:20–21).

God's last words to Israel and to the church can give us hope. May the assurance of His grace and the warnings from His love keep us living close to Him.   —DENNIS DE HAAN

What Keeps Us Going?

But whatever was to my profit I now consider loss for the sake of Christ. What is more, I consider everything a loss compared to the surpassing greatness of knowing Christ Jesus my Lord, for whose sake I have lost all things. I consider them rubbish, that I may gain Christ and be found in him, not having a righteousness of my own that comes from the law, but that which is through faith in Christ—the righteousness that comes from God and is by faith. I want to know Christ and the power of his resurrection and the fellowship of sharing in his sufferings, becoming like him in his death, and so, somehow, to attain to the resurrection from the dead. —PHILIPPIANS 3:7–11

saac Asimov tells the story of a rough ocean crossing during which a Mr. Jones became terribly seasick. At an especially rough time, a kindly steward patted Jones on the shoulder and said, "I know, Sir, that it seems awful. But remember, no man ever died of sea-sickness." Mr. Jones lifted his green countenance to the steward's concerned face and replied, "Man, don't say that! It's only the wonderful hope of dying that keeps me alive."

There's more in Jones' words than a touch of irony. As a Christian, I hear echoes of Paul's words to the Philippians. He said that the wonderful hope of dying kept him going (1:21). Yet he wasn't merely looking for relief from his suffering. Paul's hope was rooted in Christ, who died on the cross for sinners, who rose from the grave that first Easter morn, who was alive in heaven, and who would one day take Paul into His presence.

But how did the hope of seeing Christ, either at death or when He returned, keep Paul going? It gave meaning to every moment. It gave him reason to live in behalf of Christ. It also gave him incentive to focus on others who needed his encouragement. Paul had come to know Christ as his very life.

Father, thank You for the risen Christ—our reason for living. —MART DE HAAN

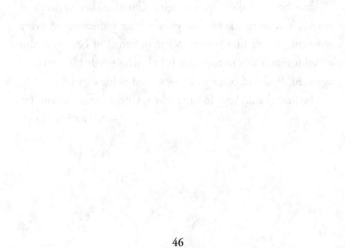

Better Times Ahead

I urge, then, first of all, that requests, prayers, intercession and thanksgiving be made for everyone—for kings and all those in authority, that we may live peaceful and quiet lives in all godliness and holiness. This is good, and pleases God our Savior, who wants all men to be saved and to come to a knowledge of the truth. For there is one God and one mediator between God and men, the man Christ Jesus, who gave himself as a ransom for all men—the testimony given in its proper time.

—1 TIMOTHY 2:1–6

Paul lived in the Roman Empire under the rule of the cruel and ruthless emperor Nero. Yet he saw the possibility of better times ahead. If he hadn't, he wouldn't have exhorted the first-century Christians to pray for "peaceful and quiet lives."

If Paul were living today, I don't think he would be pleased when Christians paint a totally dark picture of the future. Although some governments still repress their people, think of what's happened. The Berlin Wall has come down. Communism is on the wane. New winds of freedom are blowing in the world.

Yes, immorality and broken homes are still a terrible blight. But according to some observers, many people are returning to the values of marital fidelity.

I believe that the only real hope for mankind is the return of Jesus Christ. But I don't know when this event will occur. And while I wait, I'll continue witnessing for the Lord and praying for a great revival. I'll be asking the Lord to lead the nations into paths of peace and prosperity. I'll be doing what I can to help people who are struggling in dire poverty. I'll vote for leaders who uphold moral values.

We must not withdraw from the world but do what we can to make it a better place to live. God is in control. We can't lose. Let's be optimistic!

—HERB VANDER LUGT

Hope Beyond Hope

For everything that was written in the past was written to teach us, so that through endurance and the encouragement of the Scriptures we might have hope. . . .

May the God of hope fill you with all joy and peace as you trust in him, so that you may overflow with hope by the power of the Holy Spirit. —ROMANS 15:4, 13

Grant Murphy of Seattle was the active type, a man who ran at full throttle. Idling and coasting were not in his nature. "One might even call him hyperactive," remembers Paul Flint, a dear friend.

Then multiple sclerosis began to slow Grant down. First he needed crutches to get around. Then he was limited to sitting in a chair. Finally he was confined to a bed. Near the end, he was totally helpless and hardly strong enough to talk. His friend recalls, however, that "he expressed only joy and thankfulness with a constant anticipation of being in the Lord's presence."

On Paul's last visit, Grant quoted Romans 15:13 in a voice no more than a whisper. He repeated the words "as you trust in him," then added, "I can't do anything now."

It's when we can't do anything that God does everything. And herein lies a profound paradox of the Christian's experience. Faith is simultaneously an exercise of our will and the impartation of divine strength. And from that marvelous mixture spring joy and peace and an abundance of hope.

Are you in a totally helpless situation? Strength gone? All options exhausted? If you have trusted Jesus as your Savior, God will strengthen you to keep on believing. As you trust Him, He'll give you not only joy and peace but hope when all hope is gone.

—DENNIS DE HAAN

Hope Restored

The LORD upholds all those who fall
and lifts up all who are bowed down. . . .

The LORD is righteous in all his ways
and loving toward all he has made.
The LORD is near to all who call on him,
to all who call on him in truth.
He fulfills the desires of those who fear him;
he hears their cry and saves them.
The LORD watches over all who love him,
but all the wicked he will destroy.
My mouth will speak in praise of the LORD.
Let every creature praise his holy name
for ever and ever. —PSALM 145:14, 17–21

We who believe in Jesus Christ have every reason to be strong in hope. But what happens when that hope grows dim? When our circumstances or our memories or our thoughts lead us into feelings of depression or even despair? God can restore our hope.

I know, because I went through a dark episode in my life. It crept up on me gradually, unawares. As I look back now, I wonder how it ever could have happened. Finally I admitted that I was "bowed down." I could see nothing to be hopeful about. Inside, I had given up. I couldn't express it in words. I could only reach out to God for help.

God came to my rescue. His help came in several forms. Friends who had no idea what I was going through sent me encouraging notes. The two or three people I risked telling about my struggle were very supportive. My family stood with me. I received gentle, firm help from a counselor. The sunlight began to peek through the dark clouds. It became brighter as I continued to work and pray and think. I found great hope in today's verse. The Lord lifted me up.

Are you bowed down? So discouraged you feel there is no hope? Call out to the Lord for help, even if you can't put it into words. He will keep His promise. In His time, and in His way, He will lift you up. —DAVE EGNER

A Champion's Conversion

At one time we too were foolish, disobedient, deceived and enslaved by all kinds of passions and pleasures. We lived in malice and envy, being hated and hating one another. But when the kindness and love of God our Savior appeared, he saved us, not because of righteous things we had done, but because of his mercy. He saved us through the washing of rebirth and renewal by the Holy Spirit, whom he poured out on us generously through Jesus Christ our Savior, so that, having been justified by his grace, we might become heirs having the hope of eternal life.

—TITUS 3:3–7

Helene Madison was a 1932 Olympic champion. "She could outswim any woman on earth," wrote Royal Brougham of the *Seattle Post-Intelligencer*. But after winning twenty-three national championships and breaking every world record, she dropped from sight.

Thirty years later Brougham wrote a different story. He told of finding Helene sitting in a one-room basement apartment, a despondent woman. Forgotten by the world and desperately ill, the former champion was planning to drive her car to some dead-end road, close the windows, and by piping in carbon monoxide snuff out the life that still remained in her cancer-ravaged body. Brougham convinced her to change her mind and seek help.

A year later she died, but not without hope. In recounting her death, Brougham wrote, "At long last, Helene Madison placed her thin, frail hand into the hand of a bedside counselor and asked the Lord Jesus to come into her heart. She found the peace she had unsuccessfully sought in so many byways."

The same loving Savior, who gave Helene Madison peace at last, stands ready to give lasting peace and eternal salvation to all who come to God by Him.

Have you recognized your need of Christ? Has your search for peace led you to the Savior? —HENRY BOSCH

Fatal Assumption

That night all the people of the community raised their voices and wept aloud. All the Israelites grumbled against Moses and Aaron, and the whole assembly said to them, "If only we had died in Egypt! Or in this desert! Why is the LORD *bringing us to this land only to let us fall by the sword? Our wives and children will be taken as plunder. Wouldn't it be better for us to go back to Egypt?" And they said to each other, "We should choose a leader and go back to Egypt."* . . .

The LORD *said to Moses, "How long will these people treat me with contempt? How long will they refuse to believe in me, in spite of all the miraculous signs I have performed among them? . . ."*

—NUMBERS 14:1–4, 11

Tragedy can occur if we assume that a situation is hopeless when it is not. An East Detroit man made such a mistake. Thinking that he had contracted Lyme disease, he assumed that it was contagious and fatal, and that he had passed it along to his wife.

Of course, Lyme disease is neither contagious nor fatal. But because he assumed it was, he shot his wife while she was asleep and then took his own life. According to *The Detroit News*, police said the man left a note saying he felt that this was the only way out of their desperate situation.

Israel made a similar tragic mistake. Time after time God's people assumed that the Lord had led them into a blind alley of despair and that they no longer had any good choices left. Over and over they made the mistake of thinking that bad circumstances amounted to a hopelessly fatal situation. The result was that they chose desperate courses of action that resulted in the loss of their own lives and the lives of their families as well.

We need to learn from Israel's mistakes. As long as we have the ability to think and make choices, we have hope. As long as we have an opportunity to trust the Lord and wait on Him, we have an opportunity to see His ability to rescue us.

—MART DE HAAN

The God of Hope

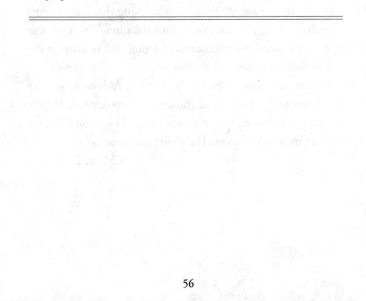

Why are you downcast, O my soul?
Why so disturbed within me?
Put your hope in God,
for I will yet praise him,
my Savior and my God. —PSALM 42:5–6

May the God of hope fill you with all joy and peace as you trust in him, so that you may overflow with hope by the power of the Holy Spirit. —ROMANS 15:13

In his book *Live with Your Emotions,* Hazen G. Werner quotes part of a letter from a woman who had run out of hope. She wrote, "A vile and ugly sin had dogged my way for years. My soul had been eclipsed in darkness. I began to feel I would never be emancipated from its grasp. Then one evening in the midst of my despair, I felt the impulse to say, 'Thank You, God, anyway,' and for a moment it was light. I said to myself, 'That must be the way.' I began to thank Him more, and the light continued and grew. For a whole evening I was relieved of my burden."

What that woman seemingly stumbled onto by accident, the psalmist had learned from experience. He found it to be a powerful truth equal to the most pressing trial. Turning the gaze of his soul heavenward, he saw God as an inexhaustible source of hope. But the psalmist's response to God was not passive. He talked to himself, challenged his downcast soul, admonished himself to hope in God, and reassured himself that he would yet praise the Lord for His help (Psalm 42:5).

Are you discouraged? Tell yourself to "hope in God." Praise Him for who He is. This could shine a ray of hope into your darkness that will lead you into the light.

—Dennis De Haan

Letdown

Suddenly a great company of the heavenly host appeared with the angel, praising God and saying,

> *"Glory to God in the highest,*
> *and on earth peace to men on whom his favor rests."*

When the angels had left them and gone into heaven, the shepherds said to one another, "Let's go to Bethlehem and see this thing that has happened, which the Lord has told us about." So they hurried off and found Mary and Joseph, and the baby, who was lying in the manger.

When they had seen him, they spread the word concerning what had been told them about this child, and all who heard it were amazed at what the shepherds said to them. But Mary treasured up all these things and pondered them in her heart. The shepherds returned, glorifying and praising God for all the things they had heard and seen, which were just as they had been told.

—LUKE 2:13–20

The night of Jesus' birth was exciting for Mary and Joseph. There before their eyes was the miracle baby whose coming into the world had been announced by an angel. The shepherds too saw and heard "a great company of the heavenly host" praising God and heralding His Son's birth (Luke 2:13). How thrilling!

But a few days later, Mary and Joseph were faced with the ordinary tasks of caring for a new baby and all the accompanying responsibilities. The shepherds were back on the hillside tending their sheep. All the elements were in place for an emotional letdown, which often follows an emotional high.

I don't believe they experienced any "after-Christmas blues," however. Mary didn't quickly forget all that had happened, and the shepherds couldn't easily forget what they had heard and seen (Luke 2:19–20). The angelic message had proven true, and their lives were filled with new hope and anticipation.

Two thousand years later, we have the full story. Jesus came to die for our sins and then conquered death for us by rising from the grave. We have more truth to ponder and more reason to glorify God than did Mary and the shepherds. We need not experience an after-Christmas letdown.

—HERB VANDER LUGT

Hope in the Sad Times

I remember my affliction and my wandering,
    the bitterness and the gall.
I well remember them,
    and my soul is downcast within me.
Yet this I call to mind
    and therefore I have hope:
Because of the Lord's great love we are not consumed,
    for his compassions never fail.
They are new every morning;
    great is your faithfulness.
I say to myself, "The Lord is my portion;
    therefore I will wait for him."
The Lord is good to those whose hope is in him,
    to the one who seeks him;
it is good to wait quietly
    for the salvation of the Lord.

—LAMENTATIONS 3:19–26

*S*adness and sorrow are life's great equalizers. They affect us all, in varying degrees.

Sometimes entire countries suffer and we are horrified by the massive sorrow we see either firsthand or on the news networks. And we are all touched by smaller-scale tragedies: accidents, illnesses, family breakups, and financial woes. Regardless of our own optimistic tendencies, sorrow visits all of us.

But there's another side to this. No matter how tragic our lives may be, no matter if we are given to depression and despair rather than happiness and joy, we are never left hopeless.

That's because life is not a string of accidental circumstances. Life has a spiritual dimension that can always be buoyed by God's love, mercy, and grace.

Look, for example, at Lamentations 3. Drenched as this passage is in the misery of the people of Jerusalem, there is hope. Amid the details of wholesale slaughter and devastation as the city was overrun, the author inserted mankind's best hope for a reason to go on: God's great love. To counter the affliction and sadness, the writer spoke of God's compassion, His faithfulness, His goodness, and His salvation (vv. 22–26).

It's remarkable! No matter what we might be suffering, we can be sure that God will never leave us hopeless.

—DAVE BRANON

Finding New Hope

I waited patiently for the LORD;
  he turned to me and heard my cry.
He lifted me out of the slimy pit,
  out of the mud and mire;
he set my feet on a rock
  and gave me a firm place to stand.
He put a new song in my mouth,
  a hymn of praise to our God.
Many will see and fear
  and put their trust in the LORD. …
Do not withhold your mercy from me, O LORD;
  may your love and your truth always protect me.
For troubles without number surround me;
  my sins have overtaken me, and I cannot see.
They are more than the hairs of my head,
  and my heart fails within me.
Be pleased, O LORD, to save me;
  O LORD, come quickly to help me.

—PSALM 40:1–3, 11–13

A woman who was widowed for the second time felt the loss deeply. She saw little reason to go on living.

One day she got into the car with her young grandson. After securing him properly, she started the car without fastening her own seatbelt. When the five-year-old politely pointed this out to her, she told him she didn't care about her safety because she wanted to go to Jesus and Grandpa. The boy replied, "But, Grandma, then you would leave me!"

God used this child to bring to her the realization that He still had service for her to perform and that her situation was not as hopeless as it seemed to be.

During almost fifty years of ministry, I've seen many despairing people come to the place where they felt there was no way out. Like Elijah, they wanted to die (see 1 Kings 19:1–18). God sustained them, however, and showed them that He still had work for them to do. They discovered that the situation was not as dark as they had thought and that God had a reason for them to go on living.

Don't give in to despair! Remind yourself of God's goodness and love. Talk to Him. He will meet your needs. He'll lead you in paths of love and light and joy where you will find new hope.

—HERB VANDER LUGT

The King Could

Then Jesus said to his disciples, "I tell you the truth, it is hard for a rich man to enter the kingdom of heaven. Again I tell you, it is easier for a camel to go through the eye of a needle than for a rich man to enter the kingdom of God."

When the disciples heard this, they were greatly astonished and asked, "Who then can be saved?"

Jesus looked at them and said, "With man this is impossible, but with God all things are possible." —MATTHEW 19:23–26

---

*L*ike many young children, I had a favorite book of nursery rhymes. I particularly remember Humpty Dumpty, pictured as a big, egg-shaped creature with a painted face and skinny arms and legs, perched happily on a wall. Then he fell and broke into countless pieces. As a child, I felt the hopelessness of the situation whenever I read that they "couldn't put Humpty Dumpty together again."

Since childhood I've come to know Christ as my Savior and Lord. I've experienced Him as the great Potter, reshaping the shattered pieces of my life and the lives of others. I've had the joy of seeing many so-called hopeless drug addicts made new in Christ. As a result, I've added a line to the Humpty Dumpty nursery rhyme: "What all the king's horses and all the king's men couldn't do, the King could!"

Are you or someone dear to you feeling shattered and broken today? Remember, no one is hopeless and beyond God's saving help. Jesus said, "With God all things are possible" (Matthew 19:26).

When the broken pieces of life seem beyond hope of repair, don't give up. We have a King who can put people back together again.   —JOANIE YODER

When You Feel Like Heman

Your word, O LORD, is eternal;
  it stands firm in the heavens.
Your faithfulness continues through all generations;
  you established the earth, and it endures.
Your laws endure to this day,
  for all things serve you.
If your law had not been my delight,
  I would have perished in my affliction.
I will never forget your precepts,
  for by them you have preserved my life.

—PSALM 119:89–93

*W*e can all relate to Heman. As we read Psalm 88, we quickly realize that things weren't going very well for him. Although he began by addressing the Lord as the One who could save him, he continued with seventeen verses of darkness.

Whenever we feel the way Heman did, we too can be honest with God. As we do that, we need to remind ourselves of the truths of the Bible that can restore our hope. Perhaps we would benefit from a new outlook that would encourage us to do the following:

Turn our attention to God (Psalm 121:1–2). One of the great ironies of trouble is that it can bring us closer to God—which is where we want to be anyway.

Praise God for our salvation (Habakkuk 3:17–18; Ephesians 1:3–8). Let's remember what the Lord has done for us through Christ. His love is far greater than any difficulty we can face.

Look for the truths that come out of affliction (James 1:2–4). A life of ease teaches less than a life of trouble and pain. We need to learn what God is trying to teach us through the struggles.

Celebrate God's faithfulness (Psalm 119:89–92). Charles Haddon Spurgeon said, "We must be tried or we cannot magnify the faithful God, who will not leave His people."

Feeling like Heman? Talk to the Lord about it. Read and meditate on the Bible passages listed above and ask Him to renew your hope. In every situation, look for the ways God is faithful—even on the darkest days. —DAVE BRANON

Hope Beyond Hope

This is what the LORD says:
"Cursed is the one who trusts in man,
    who depends on flesh for his strength
    and whose heart turns away from the LORD.
He will be like a bush in the wastelands;
    he will not see prosperity when it comes.
He will dwell in the parched places of the desert,
    in a salt land where no one lives.
"But blessed is the man who trusts in the LORD,
    whose confidence is in him.
He will be like a tree planted by the water
    that sends out its roots by the stream.
It does not fear when heat comes;
    its leaves are always green.
It has no worries in a year of drought
    and never fails to bear fruit."

—JEREMIAH 17:5–8

The English poet Alexander Pope wrote, "Hope springs eternal in the human breast: Man never is, but always to be blest." But where does man turn when hope dries up?

The director of a medical clinic told of a terminally ill young man who came in for his usual treatment. A new doctor who was on duty said to him casually and cruelly, "You know, don't you, that you won't live out the year?"

As the young man left, he stopped by the director's desk and wept. "That man took away my hope," he blurted out.

"I guess he did," replied the director. "Maybe it's time to find a new one."

Commenting on this incident, Lewis Smedes wrote, "Is there a hope when hope is taken away? Is there hope when the situation is hopeless? That question leads us to Christian hope, for in the Bible, hope is no longer a passion for the possible. It becomes a passion for the promise."

When our expectation is rooted in God and in His Son Jesus Christ as our Savior from sin and death, the blessing that Alexander Pope says we are always looking for becomes a present reality. Because God is the God of hope (Romans 15:13), He alone keeps hope flowing when its springs dry up in the human breast. —DENNIS DE HAAN

The Brightest Hope

After this I looked and there before me was a great multitude that no one could count, from every nation, tribe, people and language, standing before the throne and in front of the Lamb. They were wearing white robes and were holding palm branches in their hands. And they cried out in a loud voice:

"Salvation belongs to our God,
   who sits on the throne,
   and to the Lamb." …
Never again will they hunger;
   never again will they thirst.

The sun will not beat upon them,
   nor any scorching heat.
For the Lamb at the center of the throne will be their
    shepherd;
   he will lead them to springs of living water.
And God will wipe away every tear from their eyes."

—Revelation 7:9–10, 16–17

In the comic strip BC, a cave man stood before a rock labeled "Exchanges." He complained to the person in charge of exchanges, "My calendar watch won't budge." The other man replied, "I don't wonder. I'm not too choked up about moving into the next year myself."

We can all understand his pessimistic outlook. Tomorrow often does look dark. But the real question is: "What lies beyond midnight?"

John, the writer of Revelation, was in exile on the Island of Patmos. He wrote to people threatened with persecution for their faith. They probably weren't too eager to move into the future.

To help them, and us, face what lies ahead, John painted a picture of our ultimate future. In the presence of God, Christians will "neither hunger anymore nor thirst anymore; the sun shall not strike them, nor any heat" (Revelation 7:16). And "God will wipe away every tear from their eyes" (v. 17). What comfort that holds for us!

Someone has noted, "The only thing we know about the future is that the providence of God will be up before dawn." As we face what lies ahead, we can count on that. Hope in the God of all our tomorrows provides optimism for the future and gives strength for today.   —HADDON ROBINSON

Hopeful Derelicts

Now one of the Pharisees invited Jesus to have dinner with him, so he went to the Pharisee's house and reclined at the table. When a woman who had lived a sinful life in that town learned that Jesus was eating at the Pharisee's house, she brought an alabaster jar of perfume, and as she stood behind him at his feet weeping, she began to wet his feet with her tears. Then she wiped them with her hair, kissed them and poured perfume on them.

When the Pharisee [Simon] who had invited him saw this, he said to himself, "If this man were a prophet, he would know who is touching him and what kind of woman she is—that she is a sinner." . . .

Then he [Jesus] turned toward the woman and said to Simon, "Do you see this woman? I came into your house. You did not give me any water for my feet, but she wet my feet with her tears and wiped them with her hair. You did not give me a kiss, but this woman, from the time I entered, has not stopped kissing my feet. You did not put oil on my head, but she has poured perfume on my feet. Therefore, I tell you, her many sins have been forgiven— for she loved much. But he who has been forgiven little loves little." Then Jesus said to her, "Your sins are forgiven." . . . *"Your faith has saved you; go in peace."* —LUKE 7:36–39, 44–48, 50

Most of the men at the rescue mission service were unkempt. Some were only half awake. Not one face indicated eager anticipation as I began to speak. I thought to myself, *What can you expect? These men are skid-row alcoholics.*

But then the attitude of Jesus came to my mind, and I said, "Men, people sometimes refer to you as hopeless derelicts, but they are wrong. God sees each of you as a worthwhile person with awesome potential. He is eager to forgive you, accept you, change you, and give you eternal life."

The Pharisee in Luke 7:36–39 had a loveless attitude toward sinners that said, in essence, "Hopeless derelicts." But mature believers "regard no one according to the flesh" (2 Corinthians 5:16). To them, even the worst sinner is a potential disciple of the Lord. Through faith in Jesus anyone can be forgiven, accepted, and changed. They haven't forgotten that without Christ we would all be "hopeless derelicts."

—HERB VANDER LUGT

A Living Hope

Praise be to the God and Father of our Lord Jesus Christ! In his great mercy he has given us new birth into a living hope through the resurrection of Jesus Christ from the dead, and into an inheritance that can never perish, spoil or fade—kept in heaven for you, who through faith are shielded by God's power until the coming of the salvation that is ready to be revealed in the last time. In this you greatly rejoice, though now for a little while you may have had to suffer grief in all kinds of trials. These have come so that your faith—of greater worth than gold, which perishes even though refined by fire—may be proved genuine and may result in praise, glory and honor when Jesus Christ is revealed. Though you have not seen him, you love him; and even though you do not see him now, you believe in him and are filled with an inexpressible and glorious joy, for you are receiving the goal of your faith, the salvation of your souls. —1 Peter 1:3–9

Life is hard for everybody, but it is much harder for some than for others. Putting our trust in Christ as our Savior does little to change that. Nothing in the Bible promises us a free pass merely because we are Christ's followers. In fact, some of our wounds may not heal and some of our deficiencies may not be corrected during our lifetime. They may even get worse. Yet all of our deformities and weaknesses are only temporary.

Anticipating what God has in store for us can put a smile in our heart. Hope gives us poise and lets us live with inner strength, because we know that one day we will be dramatically different than we are now.

If you are in some way damaged by past abuse or feeling defeated by sin, or if you feel so inferior to others that you walk with your eyes to the ground, take heart in what God has in store for you. Live today with the courage God gives you. Make what you can of your afflictions. But rejoice because all that degrades and limits you is only temporary. It will be gone—some of it sooner rather than later.

If you have a living hope in Christ, you can deal with your past because of your future. God's glorious best for you lies ahead.
—HADDON ROBINSON

Seeing with Hope

Against all hope, Abraham in hope believed and so became the father of many nations, just as it had been said to him, "So shall your offspring be." Without weakening in his faith, he faced the fact that his body was as good as dead—since he was about a hundred years old—and that Sarah's womb was also dead. Yet he did not waver through unbelief regarding the promise of God, but was strengthened in his faith and gave glory to God, being fully persuaded that God had power to do what he had promised. This is why "it was credited to him as righteousness." The words "it was credited to him" were written not for him alone, but also for us, to whom God will credit righteousness—for us who believe in him who raised Jesus our Lord from the dead. He was delivered over to death for our sins and was raised to life for our justification. —ROMANS 4:18–25

Her eyes saw the leafless trees in winter, but, because Alzheimer's disease clouded her mind, she thought the trees were dead. "Someone should cut down those trees," she would repeat day after day. "They aren't coming back."

How often we see our "leafless" circumstances with a mind clouded by past experience and disappointment. We may look at a friendship, a marriage, or a family feud and say to ourselves: "Cut it down. Sever the tie. Make the break. It's hopeless!" But God wants us to see with hope because of His presence and power. We can't bring life to these seemingly impossible situations, but He can.

God's promise to Abraham that he would have a son seemed to have expired with age. Sarah his wife was barren, and his own body was "dead" at the age of 100 (Romans 4:19; Hebrews 11:11–12). Yet Abraham believed God, "who gives life to the dead and calls those things which do not exist as though they did; who, contrary to hope, in hope believed, so that he became the father of many nations" (Romans 4:17–18 NKJV).

What leafless, lifeless situation do you see today? Don't believe everything your mind tells you about it. Instead, ask God for eyes of faith that see with hope.

—DAVID MCCASLAND

Reason to Hope

I remember my affliction and my wandering,
*   the bitterness and the gall.*
I well remember them,
*   and my soul is downcast within me.*
Yet this I call to mind
*   and therefore I have hope:*
Because of the LORD's great love we are not consumed,
*   for his compassions never fail.*
They are new every morning;
*   great is your faithfulness.*
I say to myself, "The LORD is my portion;
*   therefore I will wait for him."*
The LORD is good to those whose hope is in him,
*   to the one who seeks him;*
it is good to wait quietly
*   for the salvation of the LORD.*

—LAMENTATIONS 3:19–26

*S*orrow gripped the hearts of the citizens of Jerusalem (Lamentations 1). The glorious city was in ruins and the people were facing exile. Majestic Zion had fallen to the Babylonians.

The destruction of Jerusalem in 586 BC was the result of God's judgment on an unrepentant people. Because we too can find ourselves wondering how to return to fellowship with God after failing Him, the lessons learned by those downcast citizens are worth heeding.

For the defeated people of the Holy City—and for us—the hope of restoration is given in Lamentations 3. It begins, "Yet this I call to mind, and therefore I have hope" (v. 21).

We have hope because of God's character, which is marked by these traits: His love and compassion (v. 22), faithfulness (v. 23), goodness (v. 25), and salvation (v. 26).

Although we cannot understand completely the sadness of the displaced Jerusalemites, we do know how empty life becomes when our sin cuts us off from fellowship with God. Yet we can be restored because He will forgive us when we repent of our sin. His compassions are "new every morning" (v. 23). He alone gives the refreshment of hope, and therefore we too can proclaim, "Great is Your faithfulness."

—DAVE BRANON

Prepare to Live

May the God of hope fill you with all joy and peace as you trust in him, so that you may overflow with hope by the power of the Holy Spirit. ...

Therefore I glory in Christ Jesus in my service to God. I will not venture to speak of anything except what Christ has accomplished through me in leading the Gentiles to obey God by what I have said and done—by the power of signs and miracles, through the power of the Spirit. So from Jerusalem all the way around to Illyricum, I have fully proclaimed the gospel of Christ.

—ROMANS 15:13, 17–19

In 1931, Jane Whyte felt she was nearing the end of her life. Her husband Alexander, a famous Scottish preacher, had died ten years earlier. As she looked at the world around her, she was depressed by the moral and political chaos. There seemed to be no reason for her to go on, nothing for her to do.

At dinner one evening, she sat next to a man who sensed her dejection. "What is your greatest concern?" he asked. "I'm preparing to die," said Mrs. Whyte.

"Why not prepare to live?" he suggested.

That was the question Mrs. Whyte needed to hear to break the deadlock in her life. She began to see that God wanted her to live and to touch others for Him. Her attitude changed and within a year she led a Christian outreach team on a mission to Geneva, Switzerland. That trip profoundly affected the lives of many people.

Life can seem overwhelming at times, but God offers us hope. Paul wrote, "May the God of hope fill you with all joy and peace as you trust in him, so that you may overflow with hope by the power of the Holy Spirit" (Romans 15:13).

Regardless of your age or circumstances, don't despair and "prepare to die." Believers in Christ can prepare to live—filled with, overflowing with, hope, joy, and peace.

—DAVID MCCASLAND

Do You Have Hope?

Remember that at that time you were separate from Christ, excluded from citizenship in Israel and foreigners to the covenants of the promise, without hope and without God in the world. But now in Christ Jesus you who once were far away have been brought near through the blood of Christ.

—EPHESIANS 2:12–13

I pray that out of his glorious riches he may strengthen you with power through his Spirit in your inner being, so that Christ may dwell in your hearts through faith.

—EPHESIANS 3:16–17

---

*S*everal years ago, millionaire Eugene Lang was asked to speak to a class of sixth-graders from East Harlem, New York. What could he say to inspire these students, knowing that most of them would drop out of school? Scrapping his notes, he decided to speak to them from his heart. "Stay in school," he admonished, "and I'll help pay the college tuitions for every one of you."

That was a turning point. For the first time in their lives, these students had hope. One said, "I had something to look forward to, something waiting for me. It was a golden feeling." Nearly 90 percent of that class went on to graduate from high school.

People without hope are people without a future. But when hope is restored, life is restored. This is especially true for those who come to know Christ. He gives a sure basis for hope. He has promised to return to earth to take us to our eternal home (John 14:3; 1 Thessalonians 4:17). Till then, there is help through the power of the Holy Spirit (1 Thessalonians 1:5). The believer experiences a new kind of life now and anticipates its fulfillment when Jesus returns.

Is that hope alive in your heart? If not, admit that you are a sinner. Trust Christ as your Savior. And He'll give you a hope that makes life worth living. —MART DE HAAN

Treadmill

Do not set foot on the path of the wicked
*   or walk in the way of evil men.*
Avoid it, do not travel on it;
*   turn from it and go on your way. . . .*
The path of the righteous is like the first gleam of dawn,
*   shining ever brighter till the full light of day. . . .*
Make level paths for your feet
*   and take only ways that are firm.*
Do not swerve to the right or the left;
*   keep your foot from evil.*

—PROVERBS 4:14–15, 18, 26–27

---

*I*n bad weather I get my exercise on a treadmill. But it's so boring! When the odometer says I've walked a mile, I've actually gone nowhere.

Life without God is like being on a treadmill. Generations come and generations go (Ecclesiastes 1:4). The sun rises and sets day after day, year after year (v. 5). The wind follows a repetitive course as it blows and swirls over the earth (v. 6). Rivers flow into the sea, but it is never full (v. 7). Like these natural phenomena, life is always moving but never arriving, always encountering changes but never finding anything really new. Then comes death. People without God are without hope and know they will soon be forgotten. What a dismal prospect!

How different for those who know God! Yes, they too sometimes experience routine, monotony, and difficulty, but, instead of being on a treadmill, they are on a journey. That's how Ernest Pike, an eighty-three-year-old friend of mine, viewed his life. Shortly before he died, he greeted me with a smile and said, "All my Christian life I've been preparing for heaven. Now I'm about to go there."

You too can have that hope. Admit you are a sinner. Receive Jesus as your Savior. He'll transform your life from a monotonous treadmill into a meaningful journey.

—HERB VANDER LUGT

Too Much with Us

I consider that our present sufferings are not worth comparing with the glory that will be revealed in us. The creation waits in eager expectation for the sons of God to be revealed. For the creation was subjected to frustration, not by its own choice, but by the will of the one who subjected it, in hope that the creation itself will be liberated from its bondage to decay and brought into the glorious freedom of the children of God. —ROMANS 8:18–21

William Wordsworth wrote, "The world is too much with us." He meant that too often we get caught up in the world's mad rush and fail to appreciate God's creation. But it's also easy to feel that the world is too much with us when we see people suffer for their faith in God.

The world is too much with us when we read the tragic story of a missionary family in India devastated by the murder of the father and two sons at the hands of people who hate Christians. And this world can overwhelm us when we think of the three missionary families in Colombia whose fathers and husbands were kidnapped and held for years. Added to these stories could be your own account of unjust treatment because of your faith. It happens in every country of the world.

Despite these sad situations, though, we have hope. We have the hope that comes from being God's children (Romans 8:16–17). We can call our Creator, "Abba, Father" (v. 15). We have His promise of future glory—a glory that far overshadows "our present sufferings" (v. 18).

Are the burdens of this world too much with you? Look to your heavenly Father. He lovingly offers help and hope to His struggling children.   —DAVE BRANON

Waiting

For the grace of God that brings salvation has appeared to all men. It teaches us to say "No" to ungodliness and worldly passions, and to live self-controlled, upright and godly lives in this present age, while we wait for the blessed hope—the glorious appearing of our great God and Savior, Jesus Christ, who gave himself for us to redeem us from all wickedness and to purify for himself a people that are his very own, eager to do what is good.

—TITUS 2:11–14

*I*n the 1940s, Samuel Beckett wrote a play called *Waiting for Godot,* which is now regarded as a classic. Two men stand on an empty stage, hands in their pockets, staring at each other. All they do is stand and stare. There is no action or plot. They just stand and wait for Godot to come.

But who is Godot? Is he a person? Does he represent God? Christian ethicist Lewis Smedes suggests that Godot "stands for the pipe dreams that a lot of people hang on to as an escape." As the play ends, those men are still standing on the stage doing nothing but waiting.

When the fiftieth anniversary of that play was celebrated, someone asked Beckett, "Now will you tell us who Godot is?" He answered, "How should I know?"

Waiting for Godot is a parable of many people's lives—empty and meaningless, a pointless matter of waiting. And if there's no God of love, grace, and wisdom, then life really is a hopeless waiting for empty time to pass.

How totally different, though, is Christian hope! We're waiting "for the blessed hope—the glorious appearing of our great God and Savior, Jesus Christ" (Titus 2:13). That hope sustains us—a hope that beyond this world lies a life of indescribable blessing. —VERNON GROUNDS

Remember!

When it was almost time for the Jewish Passover, Jesus went up to Jerusalem. In the temple courts he found men selling cattle, sheep and doves, and others sitting at tables exchanging money. So he made a whip out of cords, and drove all from the temple area, both sheep and cattle; he scattered the coins of the money changers and overturned their tables. To those who sold doves he said, "Get these out of here! How dare you turn my Father's house into a market!" …

Then the Jews demanded of him, "What miraculous sign can you show us to prove your authority to do all this?"

Jesus answered them, "Destroy this temple, and I will raise it again in three days."

The Jews replied, "It has taken forty-six years to build this temple, and you are going to raise it in three days?" But the temple he had spoken of was his body. After he was raised from the dead, his disciples recalled what he had said. Then they believed the Scripture and the words that Jesus had spoken.

—JOHN 2:13–16, 18–22

The disciples remembered—and then they believed. After the death of Jesus on the cross and His resurrection, they recalled and finally understood Jesus' words, "Destroy this temple, and I will raise it again in three days" (John 2:19).

If our faith is to grow, we too need to remember the cross and the empty tomb. Jesus established a memorial of His death, a practice we call the Lord's Supper, knowing that our faith and hope would be strengthened as we remember what He has done for us. He said, "Do this in remembrance of me" (1 Corinthians 11:24). Every time we meet to drink of the cup and eat the bread, we remember what it cost Him to redeem us.

The true believer does not live in memories only, however, but with hope for the future. We are to partake of the cup and bread "until he comes" (v. 26). The One who died for us also rose from the grave. As we think of our loved ones who have died in the faith, we look beyond to the day when the graves will be opened and we will meet them again. We can be sure that because Jesus lives we too shall live.

We may shed tears today in memory of those who have died. But as we recall Christ's death and resurrection, our faith and hope are renewed. Let's remember!   —M. R. DE HAAN

A Well-Founded Hope

Brothers, we do not want you to be ignorant about those who fall asleep, or to grieve like the rest of men, who have no hope. We believe that Jesus died and rose again and so we believe that God will bring with Jesus those who have fallen asleep in him. According to the Lord's own word, we tell you that we who are still alive, who are left till the coming of the Lord, will certainly not precede those who have fallen asleep. For the Lord himself will come down from heaven, with a loud command, with the voice of the archangel and with the trumpet call of God, and the dead in Christ will rise first. After that, we who are still alive and are left will be caught up together with them in the clouds to meet the Lord in the air. And so we will be with the Lord forever. Therefore encourage each other with these words.

—1 Thessalonians 4:13–18

A man in the community where I live was featured in a newspaper article because he enjoys ridiculing the Christian faith. He boldly declares his conviction that life has no meaning and that we have no basis for hope of life beyond the grave. He defiantly rejects the evidence for the existence of God and the historical record of Christ's resurrection.

The day may come when he, like the atheistic philosopher Jean-Paul Sartre (1905-1980), will long for a glimmer of hope and not be able to find it. In 1980, the ailing Sartre wrote, "Despair returns to tempt me . . . The world seems ugly, bad, and without hope. There, that's the cry of despair of an old man who will die in despair. But that's exactly what I resist. I know I shall die in hope. But that hope needs a foundation."

Within a month Sartre was dead. I wonder if he ever discovered that foundation. God's Word teaches that the only basis for hope is the empty grave and the resurrected Christ (1 Corinthians 15).

God has provided in Jesus Christ a rock-solid foundation for hope. Because He did rise from the grave, no one needs to die in despair (1 Thessalonians 4:13–14).

What about you? Is your hope founded on Christ?

—HERB VANDER LUGT

Health-Giving Hope

Therefore, prepare your minds for action; be self-controlled; set your hope fully on the grace to be given you when Jesus Christ is revealed. As obedient children, do not conform to the evil desires you had when you lived in ignorance. But just as he who called you is holy, so be holy in all you do; for it is written: "Be holy, because I am holy."

Since you call on a Father who judges each man's work impartially, live your lives as strangers here in reverent fear. For you know that it was not with perishable things such as silver or gold that you were redeemed from the empty way of life handed down to you from your forefathers, but with the precious blood of Christ, a lamb without blemish or defect. He was chosen before the creation of the world, but was revealed in these last times for your sake. Through him you believe in God, who raised him from the dead and glorified him, and so your faith and hope are in God. —1 PETER 1:13–21

*I*t is well known that our emotions can have a profound effect on our bodies. And the condition of our bodies can affect our emotions.

For example, a 1997 article in the journal published by the American Heart Association pointed to the negative physical consequences of hopelessness. It essentially said that those who had experienced extreme feelings of despair had a twenty-percent greater increase in arteriosclerosis (hardening of the arteries) over a four-year period. Other studies have also connected hopelessness with heart disease, heart attacks, and death.

The relationship between one's emotional well being and physical condition, however, is not a modern discovery. In the Old Testament book of Proverbs, we read that "a cheerful heart is good medicine" (17:22), and that the wisdom found in God's words "are life to those who find them and health to a man's whole body" (4:22).

A proper relationship to God and His Word can benefit us spiritually, physically, and emotionally. The central concern of the gospel is to bring us into a right relationship with God through faith in Christ. Its blessed by product is an abundant life filled with health-promoting hope—the assurance of total forgiveness of sins and eternal life with Christ.

—VERNON GROUNDS

"The Best Is Yet to Be"

For I am convinced that neither death nor life, neither angels nor demons, neither the present nor the future, nor any powers, neither height nor depth, nor anything else in all creation, will be able to separate us from the love of God that is in Christ Jesus our Lord. —ROMANS 8:38–39

*O*swald Chambers loved the poetry of Robert Browning and often quoted these lines from the poem "Rabbi Ben Ezra": "The best is yet to be, the last of life for which the first was made. Our times are in His hand."

As principal of the Bible Training College in London from 1911 to 1915, Chambers often said that the school's initials, B.T.C., also stood for "Better To Come." He believed that the future was always bright with possibility because of Christ. In a letter to former students written during the dark days of World War I, Chambers said, "Whatever transpires, it is ever 'the best is yet to be.'"

For the Christian, this is certainly true when we think about going to heaven. But can we believe that our remaining days on earth will be better than the past? If our hope is centered in Christ, the answer is a resounding yes!

The apostle Paul concluded the stirring eighth chapter of Romans with the assurance that nothing in the present or the future can separate us from the love of God that is in Christ Jesus our Lord (vv. 38–39). Because we are held in God's unchanging love, we can experience deeper fellowship with Him, no matter what difficulties come our way.

In Christ, "the best is yet to be."   —DAVID McCASLAND

Such a Hope

I consider that our present sufferings are not worth comparing with the glory that will be revealed in us. The creation waits in eager expectation for the sons of God to be revealed. For the creation was subjected to frustration, not by its own choice, but by the will of the one who subjected it, in hope that the creation itself will be liberated from its bondage to decay and brought into the glorious freedom of the children of God. —ROMANS 8:18–21

Two women. One a former co-worker I had known for twenty years. The other, the wife of a former student from my days as a schoolteacher. Both dedicated moms of two young children. Both missionaries. Both incredibly in love with Jesus Christ.

Then suddenly, within the space of a month, both were dead. The first, Sharon Fasick, died in a car accident, attracting little attention though deeply affecting family and friends. The second, Roni Bowers, died with her daughter Charity when their plane was shot down over the jungles of Peru—a situation that thrust her story into the international spotlight.

Their deaths filled many people with inexpressible sorrow. But there was something else—hope. Both women's husbands had the confident expectation that they would see their wives again in heaven. What happened after they died demonstrates that the Christian faith works. Both men, Jeff Fasick and Jim Bowers, have spoken about the peace God has given them. They have testified that this kind of hope has allowed them to continue on in the midst of the unspeakable pain.

Paul said that our present sufferings "are not worth comparing with the glory that will be revealed" (Romans 8:18). Such a hope comes only from Christ.　　　　　—DAVE BRANON

Restoring the Years

"Even now," declares the LORD,
    "return to me with all your heart,
    with fasting and weeping and mourning."
Rend your heart
    and not your garments.
Return to the LORD your God,
    for he is gracious and compassionate,
    slow to anger and abounding in love . . .
Then the LORD will be jealous for his land
    and take pity on his people.
The LORD will reply to them:
"I am sending you grain, new wine and oil,
    enough to satisfy you fully;
never again will I make you
    an object of scorn to the nations. . . .
"I will repay you for the years the locusts have eaten—
    the great locust and the young locust,
    the other locusts and the locust swarm—
    my great army that I sent among you.
You will have plenty to eat, until you are full,
    and you will praise the name of the Lord your God,
    who has worked wonders for you.

—JOEL 2:12–13, 18–19, 25–26

How many years have you lost to the locust? Have self-indulgence, sensuality, sinful motives, and personal ambition robbed you of joy, peace, and fruitfulness? Perhaps you feel discouraged when you think of all the time that seems to have been wasted, never to be reclaimed.

If so, consider the words of the Lord through the prophet Joel. God told the people of Israel that even though they had been disobedient to Him and had been disciplined through a plague of locusts, there was still hope. The Lord said that He is "gracious and merciful, slow to anger, and of great kindness" (Joel 2:13 NKJV). Then He promised, "I will restore to you the years that the swarming locust has eaten" (v. 25 NKJV).

When we confess our sin to the Lord, He is quick to forgive our past and fill our future with hope. He can bring good out of our wasted years. He does that by teaching us humility through our failures, and by helping us to understand the weaknesses we have in common with others.

Although our previous years may have been blighted by sin, God is eager to restore us and give us much fruit from our labor. What we have learned from the past can now result in productive service for Him and heartfelt praise to Him. The year ahead is filled with hope!   —DAVID ROPER

Beginning from the End

"May the day of my birth perish ...
I have no peace, no quietness;
    I have no rest, but only turmoil." ...
Then Job replied to the LORD:
"I know that you can do all things;
    no plan of yours can be thwarted. ...
Surely I spoke of things I did not understand,
    things too wonderful for me to know.

—JOB 3:3, 26; 42:1–3

May the day perish on which I was born.

—JOB 3:3 NKJV

At age thirty, she was ready to give up. She wrote in her diary, "My God, what will become of me? I have no desire but to die." But the dark clouds of despair gave way to the light, and in time she discovered a new purpose for living. When she died at age ninety, she had left her mark on history. Some believe that she and those who introduced antiseptics and chloroform to medicine did more than anyone to relieve human suffering in the 19th century. Her name was Florence Nightingale, founder of the nursing profession.

Job went so far as to wish he had never been born (Job 3:1–3). But thank God, he didn't end his life. Just as Florence Nightingale came out of her depression and found ways to help others, so too Job lived through his grief, and his experience has become a source of endless comfort to suffering souls.

Maybe you're at the point of not wanting to go on. Being God's child intensifies your desperation, for you wonder how a believer could feel so alone and forsaken. Don't give up. Coming to the end of yourself emotionally could be the most painful experience you've ever encountered. But take courage. Cling to the Lord in faith and start all over. God can use this kind of "beginning from the end." —MART DE HAAN

Three Needs

We know that we live in him and he in us, because he has given us of his Spirit. And we have seen and testify that the Father has sent his Son to be the Savior of the world. If anyone acknowledges that Jesus is the Son of God, God lives in him and he in God. And so we know and rely on the love God has for us.

God is love. Whoever lives in love lives in God, and God in him. —1 JOHN 4:13–16 've heard it said that there are three things a person needs to be happy:

1. Something to do—meaningful work or helping others.
2. Someone to love—someone to whom we can give of ourselves, such as a spouse, a child, or a friend.
3. Something to look forward to—a vacation, a visit from a loved one, improved health, the realization of a dream.

Those things may bring some temporary happiness. But for lasting fulfillment, these must be found in a relationship with Jesus, God's Son.

Something to do. As believers, we have been given gifts from the Holy Spirit to serve our Savior by serving others in God's family (Romans 12:1–16). We are also called to spread the gospel around the world (Matthew 28:19–20).

Someone to love. We love God because He first loved us (1 John 4:19). And we love others, "for love comes from God" (v. 7).

Something to look forward to. One day we'll be welcomed into God's presence forever, where we will enjoy a perfect place prepared especially for us (John 14:2–3; Revelation 21:3–4). We'll see Jesus and be like Him (1 John 3:2).

For lasting fulfillment, Jesus Christ truly is everything we need.

—ANNE CETAS

Strong Hands

My sheep listen to my voice; I know them, and they follow me. I give them eternal life, and they shall never perish; no one can snatch them out of my hand. My Father, who has given them to me, is greater than all; no one can snatch them out of my Father's hand. —JOHN 10:27–29

A mountain climber in the Alps had come to a treacherous place in his ascent. The only way to advance was to put his foot in the outstretched hands of the guide who had anchored himself a little way ahead of him. The man hesitated a moment as he looked below to where he would certainly fall to his death if anything went wrong. Noticing his hesitation, the guide said, "Have no fear, sir. In all my years of service my hands have never yet lost a man!"

The person who puts the destiny of his soul in Christ's hands can be sure that he will be held securely. By the Holy Spirit he is "sealed for the day of redemption" (Ephesians 4:30).

As the "author and finisher of our faith" (Hebrews 12:2 NKJV), Jesus spoke especially comforting words to His own when He said with divine finality, "They shall never perish" (John 10:28). He then underscored this promise by assuring us that we actually have double protection to keep us from being plucked from His protecting care. Christ stated that we are safe not only in His omnipotent hand but also in the Father's eternal grip (John 10:28–29).

If you have committed yourself for time and eternity into the loving care of God through faith in Christ, you need not fear. You are in His strong hands. —Henry Bosch

Reservation Guaranteed

"Do not let your hearts be troubled. Trust in God; trust also in me. In my Father's house are many rooms; if it were not so, I would have told you. I am going there to prepare a place for you. And if I go and prepare a place for you, I will come back and take you to be with me that you also may be where I am. You know the way to the place where I am going."

Thomas said to him, "Lord, we don't know where you are going, so how can we know the way?"

Jesus answered, "I am the way and the truth and the life. No one comes to the Father except through me." —JOHN 14:1–6

*B*ecause my daughter is a flight attendant, I am blessed with a parent's pass for my personal use. For a small service charge, I may fly wherever the airline flies. There's one drawback, however. I must be on "standby." That means I'm allowed on board only if there's space available. Until then, my luggage is set aside and labeled "Status Pending." While the paying passengers board, I must wait, wondering if my name will be called. I can never be certain of a seat because available space isn't guaranteed.

It's a far different situation on our journey to heaven, which begins when we trust Christ for our salvation. Because of His death and resurrection, our passage to heaven is absolutely guaranteed. Our status is *not* pending; there *is* space available; our names *will* be called. These priceless privileges have been paid for in full by the sacrificial death of Jesus.

If, like Thomas in John 14:5, you sometimes wonder if and how Jesus will get you to heaven, trust in His promise, "I go to prepare a place for *you*. And . . . I *will* come again and receive you to Myself; that where I am, there you may be also" (vv. 2–3 NKJV). That's His unfailing word. You can count on it!

—JOANIE YODER

How to Hope

*And now, dear children, continue in him, so that when he appears
we may be confident and unashamed before him at his coming.
If you know that he is righteous, you know that everyone who
does what is right has been born of him.*

*How great is the love the Father has lavished on us, that we
should be called children of God! And that is what we are! The
reason the world does not know us is that it did not know him.
Dear friends, now we are children of God, and what we will be
has not yet been made known. But we know that when he
appears, we shall be like him, for we shall see him as he is. Everyone who has this hope in him purifies himself, just as he is pure.*

—1 John 2:28–3:3

While my wife Diane was away visiting her family for a week, I got to thinking about all of the things she had asked me to fix around the house. They were improvements that had been put off for a long time. I'd been preoccupied with my own projects. But while she was gone I gained a new appreciation of her. Then it occurred to me that merely waiting and longing for her to come back was not enough. So I drew up a list of all the little jobs and got busy. Broken hardware was replaced, plants were hung, loose furniture was tightened, and dripping faucets were silenced.

As the day of her return approached, my excitement grew. In her absence I could have worked just as hard waxing the car or building shelves above my workbench—but I didn't. I knew how happy she would be, not just with the painted ceiling and the other improvements that would greet her eye, but with the change she'd see in me. I had acknowledged my past failure and had done what I knew would delight her heart.

In a similar way, we cannot expect to please Christ merely by waiting or even longing for His second coming. What counts is whether or not we care enough for Him to do something about our sins and weaknesses. That's the kind of life-changing experience spoken of in today's text. It calls for love and holy living, so that we will be ready to meet the Savior face to face. Looking forward to the day of Christ in this active way, we will learn what John meant when he wrote about a hope that purifies.

Do you know *how* to hope for Christ's return?

—MART DE HAAN

"I Will Return!"

"Men of Galilee," they said, "why do you stand here looking into the sky? This same Jesus, who has been taken from you into heaven, will come back in the same way you have seen him go into heaven." —ACTS 1:11

He who testifies to these things says,
    "Yes, I am coming soon."
Amen. Come, Lord Jesus. —REVELATION 22:20

In the early months of World War II, General Douglas MacArthur left the Philippines and fled the island of Corregidor in what seemed to be utter defeat. But when he reached Australia, he sent back this word: "I will return!" And he kept that promise. Three years later he made a second historic statement: "I have returned!"

This suggests another scene of apparent defeat. Jesus Christ came into the world and met with hostility and death. But before He left this earth, He promised to return (John 14:3). That message was given to His disciples just before He went to the cross. There He suffered what appeared to be the tragic end to His brief life of thirty-three years. Then He arose from the grave, and a short time later went to heaven. However, He immediately sent back a declaration that underscored His earlier prediction (Acts 1:11). And the very last promise in the Bible is a reiteration of this same sacred pledge (Revelation 22:20).

The second coming of Christ is called "the blessed hope" (Titus 2:13). This is especially true for the Christian, but it's also the last hope for this war-torn world. All the efforts of man to bring about a golden age of universal peace and prosperity will fail. Such blessings will be ours only when the Prince of Peace comes again to rule and reign in righteousness! We know not when He will come, but we know the event is certain.

I have on my desk a beautiful motto, sent to me by a friend in New Zealand, which reads: "Perhaps today." Yes, one of these days Christ the King of kings will return—perhaps today!

—M. R. De Haan

See You in the Morning

Because of the LORD's great love we are not consumed,
  for his compassions never fail.
They are new every morning;
  great is your faithfulness. —LAMENTATIONS 3:22–23

A dear friend of mine, David Fant, was for many years a locomotive engineer for the Southern Railway on the line between Washington, D.C., and Atlanta, Georgia. He told of one cloudy afternoon when he was at the throttle of a train heading south.

He said, "I had been somewhat depressed in spirit all day. The dark, gloomy weather on the outside seemed to correspond with the way I was feeling on the inside. We were running near the Blue Ridge Mountains when I was privileged to witness a most unusual sunset. For a few minutes the sun was bursting from behind the mountains with glorious splendor. Then suddenly it disappeared behind the towering landscape, leaving the heavens painted with a golden glow." My friend continued, "As that evening sun went down, it seemed to say, 'Good night, I will see you in the morning.' "

Immediately, Fant's mood changed and great joy filled his heart. To him, that experience became a picture of the dark age through which the Christian journeys and of the bright hope of the Savior's return.

Ever since the Son "went down" at Calvary and departed from this earth after His resurrection, the age has been steadily darkening. But before the Savior left, He promised, "I will come again." He knew all that they were going to face in the dark night before them. Yet their hearts were encouraged because they had been assured that a new and glorious day would follow. And Christians in every age have found hope in that same prospect. Yes, we will see Him in the morning!   —PAUL VAN GORDER

For Sure!

Now, brothers, about times and dates we do not need to write to you, for you know very well that the day of the Lord will come like a thief in the night. While people are saying, "Peace and safety," destruction will come on them suddenly, as labor pains on a pregnant woman, and they will not escape.

But you, brothers, are not in darkness so that this day should surprise you like a thief. You are all sons of the light and sons of the day. We do not belong to the night or to the darkness. So then, let us not be like others, who are asleep, but let us be alert and self-controlled. … He died for us so that, whether we are awake or asleep, we may live together with him. Therefore encourage one another and build each other up, just as in fact you are doing.

—1 Thessalonians 5:1–6, 10–11

As my wife and I looked forward to having our second baby, we took advantage of some childbirth classes offered by the hospital. One segment of the course sticks in my mind. It was a film that attempted to relieve the fears that can be so unsettling to expectant parents. A long series of questions were posed. When will your labor begin? Will you be at home? Will there be plenty of time to get to the hospital? Will your delivery be hard? And what about your baby? Can you expect a boy or a girl? Will it be large or small? Will it be healthy?

The narrator then summed it up something like this: "Yes, there are so many questions left unanswered. But one thing is sure. You will deliver. You will give birth!" The class laughed. To a group of such visibly expectant mothers and their husbands, that final conclusion couldn't have been more obvious. Yet its realism was comforting to us all.

The whole experience reminded me of the Lord's second coming mentioned in our Scripture reading. There are so many questions that come to mind. What will it be like? Will it be a startling experience? Will we be happy when we see Him? Where will we be when it occurs? Will we be living, or will we be among those who are raised from the dead? Yes, as we anticipate the birth of that new day, there are still some unanswered questions. But one thing we can all be sure of—He is coming again! Even though we don't see Him now, our eyes will behold Him then. We will be as ready as our faith, hope, and love have prepared us to be.

—MART DE HAAN

Dirty Windows

Brothers, we do not want you to be ignorant about those who fall asleep, or to grieve like the rest of men, who have no hope. We believe that Jesus died and rose again and so we believe that God will bring with Jesus those who have fallen asleep in him. According to the Lord's own word, we tell you that we who are still alive, who are left till the coming of the Lord, will certainly not precede those who have fallen asleep. For the Lord himself will come down from heaven, with a loud command, with the voice of the archangel and with the trumpet call of God, and the dead in Christ will rise first. After that, we who are still alive and are left will be caught up together with them in the clouds to meet the Lord in the air. And so we will be with the Lord forever. Therefore encourage each other with these words.

—1 THESSALONIANS 4:13–18

The Shepherd's Home in Wisconsin has a problem with dirty windows. Although many of its residents are severely disabled, they love Jesus and understand that He has promised to return someday and give them new bodies. "Every day," said the superintendent, "some of them go to the windows and press their noses against the glass, looking for Him."

The expectation of those precious people is genuine. Their irreversible mental and physical limitations fuel their longing for the day when they will be perfectly whole and free.

The Holy Spirit enables us to keep alive that same hope. And it is a sure hope because it rests on two events, one past and one future: the resurrection of Jesus Christ from the dead (1 Corinthians 15:20), and the reality that He will return to this earth someday (1 Thessalonians 4:13–18).

When the going gets tough, we must resist the temptation to give up on life, or to find morbid pleasure in complaining. Instead, we must stay obedient to the Lord, renounce sin, and keep our eyes on the future (1 Corinthians 15:33–34). Then we can rejoice in the certainty that in the world to come our painful trials will be no more.

Let's keep looking for Christ's return.

—DENNIS DE HAAN

Hope for the World
Renewed Hope

Fight the good fight of the faith. Take hold of the eternal life to which you were called when you made your good confession in the presence of many witnesses. In the sight of God, who gives life to everything, and of Christ Jesus, who while testifying before Pontius Pilate made the good confession, I charge you to keep this command without spot or blame until the appearing of our Lord Jesus Christ, which God will bring about in his own time—God, the blessed and only Ruler, the King of kings and Lord of lords, who alone is immortal and who lives in unapproachable light, whom no one has seen or can see. To him be honor and might forever. Amen. —1 TIMOTHY 6:12–16

PEACE TALKS FALL APART AGAIN.
UNEMPLOYMENT RATE RISES.
TORNADO RIPS THROUGH TOWN.

These newspaper headlines selected at random tend to lead us to despair. There just doesn't seem to be any hope for this world. And yet, according to the Scriptures, the dream of abolishing war is not merely wishful thinking. The idea of prosperity for all is more than a political gimmick. The Bible tells us that the eventual taming of nature is a certainty.

The hope for this world, however, is not to be found in human efforts but in the return of Jesus Christ. He alone can solve the problems that are baffling mankind.

The prophet Isaiah said that someday "nation will not take up sword against nation, nor will they train for war anymore" (Isaiah 2:4). This glorious prospect will become a reality when the Lord Jesus Himself returns as "King of kings and Lord of lords" (1 Timothy 6:15) to set up His kingdom of peace and righteousness. We are to be "looking for the blessed hope and glorious appearing of our great God and Savior Jesus Christ" (Titus 2:13 NKJV). Because we have this hope, we can be optimistic even in the deepening gloom of this age.

Keep looking up!   —RICHARD DE HAAN

About the Authors

Henry Bosch served as the first editor of the daily devotional booklet that became *Our Daily Bread* (ODB) and contributed many of the earliest articles. He was also one of the singers on the Radio Bible Class live broadcast.

Dave Branon has done freelance writing for many years and has published more than thirteen books. Dave taught English and coached basketball and baseball at the high school level before coming to RBC Ministries (RBC), where he is now the Managing Editor of *Sports Spectrum* magazine.

Anne Cetas is Assistant Managing Editor on the editorial staff at RBC Ministries and has been with the ministry for twenty-five years. Anne and her husband Carl also work as mentors in an inner-city ministry. "It's the most challenging ministry I've ever loved," says Anne. She also teaches Sunday school and disciples new believers.

Dennis De Haan is a nephew of RBC founder, Dr. M. R. De Haan. He pastored two churches in Iowa and Michigan before joining the RBC staff in 1971. He served as Associate Editor of ODB from 1973 until 1982 and then as Editor until June 1995. Now retired, Dennis continues editing for ODB on a part-time basis.

Mart De Haan is the grandson of RBC founder, Dr. M. R. De Haan, and the son of former president, Richard W. De Haan. Having served at RBC for over thirty years, Mart is heard regularly on the *Discover the Word* radio program and seen on *Day of Discovery* television. Mart is also a contributing writer for ODB, the Discovery Series Bible study booklets, and a monthly column on timely issues called "Been Thinking About."

Dr. M. R. De Haan was the founder of Radio Bible Class and one of the founders of *Our Daily Bread*. A physician who later in life became a pastor, he was well known for his gravelly voice and impassioned Bible teaching. His commitment to ministry was to lead people of all nations to personal faith and maturity in Christ. The Grand Rapids, Michigan-based RBC Ministries continues to build upon the spiritual foundation of Dr. De Haan's vision and work.

Richard De Haan was President of RBC Ministries and teacher on RBC programs for twenty years. He was the son of RBC founder, Dr. M. R. De Haan, and wrote a number of full-length books and study booklets for RBC. Often called "the encourager," Richard was committed to faithfulness to God's Word and to integrity as a ministry. His favorite expression was "Trust in God and do the right." Richard went to be with the Lord in 2002.

Dave Egner is now retired from RBC. He was (until June 2002) Managing Editor of *Campus Journal*. He has written Discovery Series study booklets and articles for a variety of publications. Dave taught English and writing for ten years at Grand Rapids Baptist College (now Cornerstone University) before coming to RBC.

Vernon Grounds, Chancellor of Denver Seminary, has had an extensive preaching, teaching, and counseling ministry and was president of Denver Seminary. In addition to writing articles for ODB, he has also written many books and magazine articles.

David McCasland researches and helps develop biographical documentaries for *Day of Discovery* television, in addition to writing

ODB articles. His books include the award-winning biography *Oswald Chambers: Abandoned to God,* a compilation of *The Complete Works of Oswald Chambers,* and *Pure Gold,* a biography of Eric Liddell.

Haddon Robinson is the discussion leader for the RBC Ministries' *Discover the Word* radio program, in addition to writing for *Our Daily Bread.* Dr. Robinson teaches at Gordon-Conwell Theological Seminary, where he is the Harold J. Ockenga Distinguished Professor of Preaching. He has authored several books, including *Biblical Preaching* and *Biblical Sermons,* which is currently used as a text for preaching in 120 seminaries and Bible colleges throughout the world.

David Roper was a pastor for more than thirty years and now directs Idaho Mountain Ministries, a retreat dedicated to the encouragement of pastoral couples. He enjoys fly-fishing, fly-tying, hiking, and just being streamside in the mountains with his wife Carolyn. He is the author of eleven books, including *Psalm 23: The Song of a Passionate Heart.*

Paul Van Gorder began writing regularly for ODB in 1969 and continued until 1992. He also served as associate Bible teacher for the *Day of Discovery* television program and traveled extensively as a speaker for Radio Bible Class. He and his wife now live in retirement in South Carolina.

Herb Vander Lugt is Senior Research Editor for RBC Ministries and has been at RBC since 1966. In addition to ODB articles, he also writes Discovery Series booklets and reviews all study and devotional materials. Herb has pastored six churches, and since retiring from the pastorate in 1989, has held three interim pastor positions.

Joanie Yoder, a favorite among ODB readers, went home to be with her Savior in 2004. She and her husband established a Christian rehabilitation center for drug addicts in England many years ago. Widowed in 1982, she learned to rely on the Lord's help and strength. She wrote with hope about true dependence on God and His life-changing power.